Inspiration and Provocation for More
Creative Meetings and Workshops

———

Contents

There's No Right Way

There's no right order of learning, or meeting.

The world is made up of intelligent networks—think of the internet, or a good ecology, or your brain. In these, the "wiring" is messy so that things are connected in a myriad of ways.

There is no single, right order. No one path through the swamp.

So in this second edition of our book, we're sharing our ideas as a series of short reflections and we invite you to read them in any order you like.

Different people will want to make sense of these pages in different ways, and it's not for us to second-guess your unique and unpredictable intelligence.

There will be ideas in this book that make immediate sense to you and some that don't. Some may seem to contradict each other.

Not every explanation will feel complete, because we're not aiming to write a simple how-to guide. This is not a book of techniques, although we occasionally describe some processes. (We do list a whole heap of processes at our website here: creativefacilitation.com/resources)

When we run workshops, we often use this book just once. We rip off the binding, and give each participant just one page to read. And then we get people to pair off several times and share what they learn with each other. This is a more sociable process for sharing information—and confirms that you don't need to read this book in a linear order.

There's a parallel here for our work as facilitators. We're wary of efforts to closely structure the order of the events we're hosting. We find, again and again, that our best work is improvised, created in the moment in response to what's happening live in the room. Changes of pace and direction are signs of life, not disorder. Having too rigid a plan stops us from seeing new connections as they emerge.

It's Not Meant To Be Easy

Relaxing in the face of difficulty without oversimplifying.

The trouble with the word "facilitation" is that people think our job is to make things easy. That can be a trap, because we often ask people to work on things that are charged with emotion and full of complexity. If we act as if this stuff is simple, we're likely to look foolish.

Instead, we prefer to think of facilitation as "bringing a sense of ease to difficult things." We acknowledge the challenge we're asking people to work with and we embody an attitude that allows for more reflection, creativity and ability to see unexpected connections.

One of the most frequent things we practice when people get anxious or we feel pressure, is to remember to breathe, relax and maintain physical calm. It almost always helps.

Meetings Don't Have To Suck

There can be something magical about meeting in person—whether it's a friend you haven't seen for a long time or your work colleagues.

It's the human sharing, the energy, the connection that we crave. It is in these face-to-face meetings that creativity and innovation flourish, where ideas can abound, where we meet new people, make and reinforce relationships and build a platform for our own work.

Yet most people seem to dread meetings, and we all know the temptations to drift off to look at our devices as familiar voices say familiar things.

It doesn't have to be this way. Our job is to take risks to disrupt the boredom and bad habits that stop people connecting and working together.

Why Would A Group Need A Facilitator?

A facilitator brings an understanding of human interaction and how to make the most of valuable time spent together.

A facilitator can be a part of, or apart from, the group. In either case, the role is a special one. A facilitator is concerned about the overall flow of a meeting or workshop, encouraging participation, surfacing dissenting views, encouraging listening and dialogue, and building connections and meaning.

Facilitation processes and activities are all about participation—giving everyone in a group, meeting or workshop, an opportunity to contribute. The facilitator provides only a portion of this transaction. Group members also have a responsibility to choose the level and type of their participation.

Here are some of the situations we've been asked to facilitate.

✓ **Something's going wrong and they don't know what it is**
They just can't work out what's wrong, but they know something is. When people are so much a part of the group it's hard for them to see what is happening or to be objective about it.

✓ **The group needs to prepare for change**
Restructuring, a new boss, change in operating procedures, a merger, there can be so many changes on the horizon and the group needs to be agile, flexible, and ready to respond to any number of changes and developments.

✓ **The group needs to make decisions**
It's appropriate for the group to make a joint decision. They want to get everyone involved, hear diverse, even contrary views, and reach a point where a decision is possible, or if not, to identify what needs to be done to make one later.

✓ **The group needs to work differently**
There's nothing wrong per se, but the sponsor wants the group to work differently—step up, slow down, take care of each other, be braver—there's no end of possibilities for exploring how to work differently.

✓ **The group wants to learn from each other's experiences**
No matter what the scenario, this is a common reason for bringing groups together to reflect on a shared experience, identify what worked well and what didn't and what improvements can be made.

✓ **The group is stuck**
Treading water, not doing badly, but not improving or doing well either—maybe stuck in ways of working that are no longer suitable, unable to make a decision, or feeling a bit bored.

What Is It That You Do Again?

Facilitation is like slow-motion multi-tasking.

Challenge habits of thinking and acting

A workshop is meant to provide a break from normal routine. So it's unlikely to satisfy if the same thinking and routines used in the workplace are simply moved to a workshop setting. Facilitators challenge habits and help groups to experience different ways of thinking and acting together.

Hold space

For new thinking to emerge, we have to get outside our comfort zones - facing challenging questions, sitting with anxiety or frustration, waiting for solutions rather than forcing them. A facilitator is partly responsible for holding space: supporting an atmosphere in which there's room for the new to safely emerge.

Model behaviours

There's a lot more going on in a group than just talking. People pick up the attitudes and behaviours of others and often copy what they see or hear.

Notice and reflect back

Acting on behalf of the group, a facilitator can notice what's happening—not judging, not interpreting, not analyzing—just noticing and stating what is observed. This can be important for a group that is usually too busy doing to ever notice itself or others. Some of the most effective interventions occur when a facilitator (merely) offers an observation describing what is happening in the room.

Look for opportunities to get out of the way

A facilitator will start an activity, then get out of the way and let the group get on with it. People often don't need more instructions, information, processes, details or help. They just need the time and space to get on with it.

Select appropriate activities and processes

There is no shortage of facilitation processes. Don't believe anyone who says their process is 'the one'. The art of facilitation is knowing what's out there, and what to use in any given situation. There's no shortcut to learning this—it comes from experience. And the only way to get that experience is to facilitate.

Provide a suitable environment/space

It may seem unimportant, but the space in which people work can affect the quality of their work. When working with a group, facilitators make the best use of available space and look at each working environment with fresh eyes, deciding what's needed and what's not. At the very least, one simple thing you can do to improve the space is to remove the tables. Most workshops benefit from access to wall space and floor space, natural light and the outdoors.

Keep track of time and progress

While facilitation is far more than just time-keeping, it is still an important aspect. Time-keeping is more about being attuned to the needs of the group rather than planning for, and strictly adhering to, an agenda. It's about allowing more time when needed, stopping something that's not working, calling breaks when people need a break, and finishing on time.

Support the group by clarifying, questioning, sometimes challenging and summarising

It's not necessary to be an expert in the subject or the work of the group to be a good facilitator. There is no hard and fast rule. Sometimes it's helpful to know about the topic, but often not. What is needed is a keen sense of knowing that something just doesn't seem right - more of an instinct than an actual knowing. Or a sense that participants are saying what they think they should be saying rather than what they actually want to say or what they are really thinking. Or that they are using jargon or 'organisational' speak as a way of glossing over and not engaging with the topic being discussed. In all of these situations, the facilitator will ask for clarification, even challenge people to say what they really mean. A facilitator can also say what others cannot: "I don't know", "I don't understand", "Tell me more".

Sometimes we admit we don't know what to do

Yes, you read that correctly. Sometimes we have no idea what to do next. As usual, there is no rule about what to do when you don't know what to do. We might call a break—maybe our brain just needs a rest. We might tell the group and ask their advice. Or we might trust our intuition and start something knowing that something will emerge.

(Thanks to Tim Harford for inspiring the idea of slow-motion multitasking.)

Expect Creative People

A few of the mantras we live by...

Design for talented participants

One of the most common questions we get asked about working with groups is how to deal with difficult people. The longer we've been doing this, the fewer of these difficult people we run into.

We design meetings on the assumption that the participants will be smart, wise and creative. We find that when we do this, these are the kinds of people who show up.

Fun and work are not mutually exclusive

Important and serious are not the same. You can do important work in many different ways, one of which is seriously. You can also have fun with serious work. A facilitator knows the difference between important and serious, between fun and frivolity—and chooses appropriately.

Talk is action

Some people are so busy proving how busy they are that they forget the substance of human connection—conversations and relationships. If organisations and businesses want to be resilient and responsive they need to value the time and energy it takes to build and nurture relationships, both within and outside of the business, that will weather the good and bad times. Having a conversation is doing something—something important, necessary and nourishing.

The group has the knowledge

A group of people working together will spark off each other, share what they know, build on each other's ideas. They have the knowledge and experience they need. Sometimes it's good to inject something new as a catalyst, or to motivate or challenge the group, but this is just another part of the facilitator's challenge. It's the participants who can put the puzzle pieces together in a way that is relevant and useful for them.

Everybody has something to contribute

Facilitators know how to encourage quieter voices to be heard, and believe that everyone, loud and quiet, has something to contribute.

Meaning emerges

Life is messy. Work is messy. Solutions, ideas, and insights may not be easily accessible or discernable. It may take time and a number of approaches for meaning to emerge.

What Sort Of Facilitator Are You?

Facilitators bring personal qualities to their work that serve them and the people they work with.

Humble

This is recognising the power you have as a facilitator and letting it go. Being comfortable to spend some of the time on the sidelines, not being the centre of attention, recognising the ideas that emerge from others. Humility also asks that you suspend judgment and not jump to conclusions. Humility is not piety though - the word's origins are from the Latin for earth, suggesting groundedness.

Empathetic but not pathetic

The ability to "read the room"—having a sense of how participants are responding—is possibly the most important quality in a facilitator. When people believe you're correctly sensing how they feel, and are willing to acknowledge it, it does more for their sense of safety than any list of ground rules.

But let's not kid ourselves: we're not mind readers. It's often good to check out our hunches. And we also need to avoid getting trapped in one of the most painful stereotypes of facilitation: becoming a fusspot, nannying the group and labouring how much we care for them. Sometimes we need to set boundaries and act.

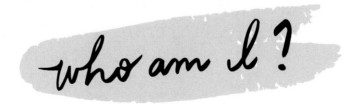

Warrior mode

Taking risks, disrupting traditional or typical patterns of thinking or behaviour requires strength, especially when it goes against the norms of meetings, the expectations of clients and participants, and the urge to conform or be safe. It requires bravery to break the rules and change the game. Not everything works but that doesn't mean we need to always be tentative in what we do.

Facilitators need to be willing to try, to fail, to move on and try something else. Without a willingness to fail it's difficult to be disruptive in service to the group. Playing it safe is like running on the spot—you and the group rarely progress. Some of the most encouraging feedback we get from clients is that we seem to make good judgements about when to step forward and intervene, and when to fade into the background and stay out of the way.

Playful

We have difficult, complex problems to deal with. This doesn't mean that it can't be done lightly and playfully. Play involves imagination and creativity, often suspending "rules" and stepping outside of expectations. Playfully exploring our most difficult questions can lead us to surprising results.

A Network Model Of Meetings

Treat your meeting more like a network than a hierarchy, and unleash it's creative power.

Are you running your meetings—and your organisation—like a hierarchy or as an intelligent network?

This diagram was originally produced in the 1960s to describe different kinds of network. This could be an energy system, an airline route map or a computer network.

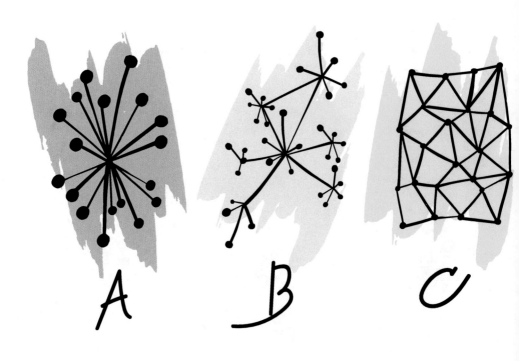

We can also use this diagram to look at how we run meetings. Many meetings follow plan A—one person speaks, and everyone else listens. Your average powerpoint presentation is like this. If you have a Q and A session, or a big plenary session, the person everyone listens to changes (briefly) but the essential model is the same.

We might switch to plan B, with small breakout conversations chaired by a host. These then report back to the centre. This seems to offer more scope for conversations, but it can be quite restrictive in its own way. And the report-backs from breakout groups can be stilted and slow—creeping death.

The idea of meeting like network C makes many organisers panic. All sorts of connections can happen, but it looks messy and it's hard to stay in control of all the information.

But C is a network designed for robustness. And of the three, it's the one that most closely resembles the way a brain works (albeit in a highly simplified way). For meetings, it's more likely to generate new ideas, and to maintain the engagement and enthusiasm of participants. It's essentially a model that allows for more aliveness.

This diagram represents a freeze frame of a network, the real thing is actually much more dynamic. So are your meeting participants—but are you willing to let them be?

If you are willing to break away from convention, there are lots of ways to allow participants in your meetings to create connections more freely, acting as their own agents and not being controlled from the centre. Approaches like Open Space allow participants to set their own agendas for breakout conversations. Introductory activities can encourage people to identify individual knowledge, interests and concerns, and form small conversations with others on that basis. By using more distributed methods, you increase the number of possible connections people can make, and allow them to meet more personally, rather than from behind a lectern or in a rushed question to a keynote speaker. You can find lots of ways to give participants real agency in choosing who to talk to, and have an event characterised by lively conversations, rather than familiar monologues.

It's not as controlling but it's more liberating.

When To Back Away Slowly

Sometimes you don't need a facilitator.

Sometimes people ask for a facilitator when what they really need is a master of ceremonies, or a moderator, or a timekeeper, or someone to keep everyone 'in line' and pleasant with each other despite an undertow of simmering emotions.

Many of the techniques of facilitation can be used to manipulate people, and to create the illusion that you are in control. Sometimes facilitation can default to searching for the 'one right answer'. Sometimes it has even been predetermined. We don't want to facilitate if a decision has already been made, or when management wants the group to come up with the same 'answer' they have already chosen. We call this kind of work "facipulation". Trying to facilitate in these situations just gives facilitation a bad name.

Beyond Polite

Finding a field for dialogue.

In his book, *Dialogue*, William Isaacs notices that in many meetings people engage in polite conversations, which sometimes move to skilled argument. It is possible for groups to go deeper than this, where people are willing to explore openly what is the thinking that lies behind the positions they take.

Isaacs suggests that when we meet, we create a field together... a kind of collective mindset or energy within which our conversations take place. Most conversations begin with politeness, we speak of our own experience and don't get drawn into where that clashes with others. There might be a shift to argument, what Issacs calls breakdown when we argue our positions. Many conversations stay within these two fields. But it is possible to move beyond these into deeper territory where we defend less and explore more, reflecting on our thinking rather than just doing it. This requires some skillful and attentive facilitation—the first step, as always, is being aware of what is going on for the group, and providing ample opportunity and time for deeper conversations.

The People Are The Content

Your participants are smarter than your processes.

When planning events, it's easy to focus on the content that is going to be discussed and presented. A lot of time can be spent second-guessing how people will react to the materials and ideas being set before them.

We like to remind ourselves that the people are the content, a thought we first heard from our friend, Rob Poynton.

Each participant arrives with their own experiences and ideas. They bring vast and varied thoughts, concerns and knowledge. This amounts to vastly more intelligence than can ever be compressed into a motivational speech, a powerpoint or a briefing document. They need to connect to each other to realise their potential.

We nearly always experience relief and aliveness as events start and real human beings come into the room. Only then do we really feel connected to what we are really going to be working with. It's a completely different energy and mindset than that of planning and worrying.

Antony Williams suggests there are three things people want from meetings: ***Identity, Connection and Action.***

 Identity: we want our own identify affirmed. At its most basic level, we want people to know our name, and to have our own thoughts and views acknowledged.

 Connection: we don't come to meetings to be alone. We want to feel connection, and we may already have some known and unknown connections with others in the group.

 Action: People want something to happen, for there to be movement and change.

We thought about this three part model playing one of our favourite introductory activities in Cambridge recently. We had a group of about 20 people who'd never met before, so we played a name game. This is a ball throwing game in which we practice naming all the other participants. It's done in a playful spirit that's highly accepting of mistakes.

We all stood in a circle and called our (first) names in turn. Then someone would start by throwing an imaginary ball to someone else in the circle, saying their (first) name. Sometimes this might be a bit of a guess from memory, sometimes it was done with certainty. The person thrown to would that state their own name before throwing the ball to someone else.

The brief for this game is to not get stuck on mistakes. So if you're thrown the ball by someone who says your name wrong, you don't stop the game to scold them, you act as if this all fine and simply state your correct name on receipt and throw it to the next person.

We know from experience that getting the names right is not as important as keeping the energy flowing. Stopping to agonise before throwing doesn't create satisfaction. Whereas a lightly held mistake can be taken playfully.

As with all these apparently trivial games, a lot goes on and it reminded us of Antony's model. If players focus too hard on their identity, they stop the game when someone says their name wrong. If they worry about action—making progress— they worry too much about the mistakes and become distracted. But as the game progresses, we realise that we are learning everyone's name and feeling quite energised.

In organisations, the pressure for results means we easily skip over connection—but without it, we may be failing to create the kind of group spirit that leads to much better communication and insight.

It's Not About You

As facilitator, you are pivotal, but it's not about you.

Being able to hold this paradox is one of the skills of a facilitator—to be in service of the group and the work they need to do AND to show humility, respect and recognise that by your very presence you are also a part of the group.

The processes you use as a facilitator are the just scaffolding that supports the building of a robust, resilient, capable team or group who will proceed, without you, to do their work—whatever that is.

One of our best learning experiences came when we worked with an international team using some improv activities. We demonstrated a theatre game designed to build skills for responding to unexpected events. We had a feeling that people just weren't getting it but decided to let them work in small groups for a time. Apart from anything else, we needed a bit of time to confer.

We sat in a corner of the room in an anxious discussion about why this activity wasn't really working and what could we do to get things going better. This took some time because we knew we had to come up with something to save the day.And then we looked up. While we had been sweating, the little groups of participants had become hugely animated, and they were happily doing the work with gusto and skill. We looked at each other and laughed: it was not the participants that needed a lesson—it was us who needed to just get out of people's way and give them time to work on their own.

Be Aware Of What Your Body Is Telling You

If you are not connecting with yourself it's much harder to connect with others.

Gut feelings often get a bad rap in favour of logical, evidence-based decision-making. When learning to facilitate there can be an over-emphasis on cognitive, thinking-based approaches. There's no doubt that thinking is important. It's only a problem if it's the only thing you rely on. Thinking is a chemical process that happens in your brain. Sometimes your brain is awash with chemicals triggered from somewhere else in your body and you feel it before you know it. Take notice of what your body is telling you. The fancy word for this is interoception.

For example, if you forget what to say, stop. Say nothing. Keep breathing. Your brain will catch up. Sometimes you might notice when you feel anxious and have forgotten something, you will realise that you're not breathing. Literally, you hold your breath. Without oxygen the brain can't work properly, so keep breathing.

Sometimes facilitators will tell us that they feel nothing in their bodies. More likely, they have lost touch with the feelings in their bodies. Part of the skill of noticing is training yourself to notice even subtle changes in your body—a tightening of your diaphragm, tenseness in your shoulders, butterflies in your stomach, heaviness in your arms or legs. These are all signals and can be very helpful in responding.

If you are not connecting with yourself it's much harder to connect with others.

Step Into Your Fear

Anxiety and excitement are very close. Is that feeling in your stomach nerves or excitement?

Actors, presenters, performers of all sorts will say they feel nervous before they begin, no matter how experienced they are. It's the same for facilitators. Some nerves are good—they sharpen our senses, remind us that we're alive, prime us to perform.

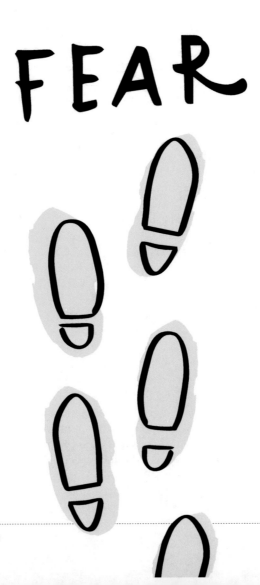

Sometimes It Sucks

There has to be an easier way to make a living, right?

Sometimes, this work hurts and we might leave a meeting feeling upset, telling ourselves we got it wrong, or could have done better. We're only human. A good debrief with a colleague or friend who's good at listening can help a lot.

Working With Emotions

Emotions are a part of being human.

Sometimes we might hear someone say, "Let's keep the emotion out of the argument". It is a myth that we can make decisions, work together, resolve problems, and collaborate without emotions getting in the way. Not true. We humans are emotional beings. We might try and hide our emotions but they will leak out. Our emotions also provide us with valuable information, and it can be a relief to let go and express our emotions. If we hold them (or try to control them) too tightly, it can stop us from feeling anything at all, including empathy.

Equally, facilitation is not therapy. You are not there to provide catharsis, or help people solve their personal problems, or surface their demons, or deal with their neuroses. If this happens as a consequence of group activities or processes, then that's all right. But it's not, and never should be, the main game.

Because most of us carry our own uncertainties and demons with us, strong emotions might emerge during a workshop. What should you do? How should you deal with them?

Here are some things that work for us.

✓ Hold a space for emotions

Don't react—just allow the emotions (yours and others) to emerge and play out. Be present and alert.

✓ Avoid finger-pointing, fixing and rescuing

Many people are uncomfortable with strong emotions, for all sorts of reasons. Some people respond with inappropriate comments or humour. Others try to 'fix' or 'rescue' the person or situation. Gently resist these tendencies in yourself or in others, and continue to hold the space for emotions.

✓ Acknowledge and move on

Try not to make a big deal about emotional responses—they are another part of working with humans. Acknowledge and move on, but only when the group is ready to do so. You might discover that an 'emotional outburst' surfaces some underlying issue that needs to be dealt with. Or it might not. There are no rules.

✓ Do more of what works

In workshops, you are likely to encounter loud, dominating types, as well as quiet, reserved types, and even passive-aggressive types. Our approach is not to categorise people—people are usually far more complex than that and categorisation doesn't help very much—or to single out 'difficult' people. What we do is notice what is happening and use some, or all, or none of the approaches we've described: listening, paying attention, shifting status, introducing an activity to potentially surface buried emotions, varying our approach. In short, there's no recipe for dealing with difficult people or moments. We notice. We act. We notice what is working and what is not. So we can do more of what works, and if something is not working, we try something else. Sometimes the smallest of shifts can have the greatest effect.

Unhurried

Unhurried is the pace we set for what we need to do - it's neither fast nor slow.

Sometimes we think the most important thing we can do in meetings is to pay attention to time and pace. It's why we often use the word "unhurried" to describe our approach. In fact, we made a whole website exploring and applying this idea at unhurried.org.

Rather than repeat what's on that site, we'll just share this story:

We were hosting a meeting where we ran out of time because of an emergency meeting everyone had to rush off to. The two-hour session we'd planned was down to a ridiculous 25 minutes. These are the kinds of situation where we've trained ourselves to relax and wait to see what the opportunity is.

The pressure was added when the group said it wanted to use this time to develop a vision! On the face of it, a crazy demand - that stuff can take forever. But we trusted their wisdom and thought, well what can we do?

First, we acknowledged how little time we had, so suggested we can only do our best, make a start and see where we get. It's really useful to signal this to the group

Then we asked each of the eight participants to write, on their own, a bad first draft of a vision statement. We stopped all questions and statements and discussion and said, "just write". We spared everyone a potentially long discussion about the differences between visions and missions. We decided just to start anywhere.

After about five minutes, everyone had some kind of draft. Some were full paragraphs, others were just random words. Ok, it seemed like enough. So we decided to pair people up and told each pair to combine their two statements into one. They seemed willing to try this, and while they worked we had a little more time to think about what the next stage would be. Of course, we didn't really know what sort of output we'd get from the pairs, so we just daydreamed alternatives.

After five minutes, we asked each pair to read out their shared statements. Some hadn't written anything and just talked about what they'd discussed. Others had cobbled together a few key words. One pair, as it turned out, had managed a fairly coherent 50 words. As they read it out, we noticed that many of the other participants were nodding and making approving noises.

So we asked, do we all think this is an okay draft to work on? The answer was yes. So in that moment, we suggested that the pair write their draft up on a flip chart, and as they did so, everyone spontaneously gathered round in a lively discussion. Various marker pens were fielded, some crossing-out happened and some words were added. Our role at this point was to do nothing. The group was working.

Then we noticed we were just about out of time, so we said, does this feel like a good starting point for further work on the vision? Again, everyone seemed happy.

So we said, great, we're finished.

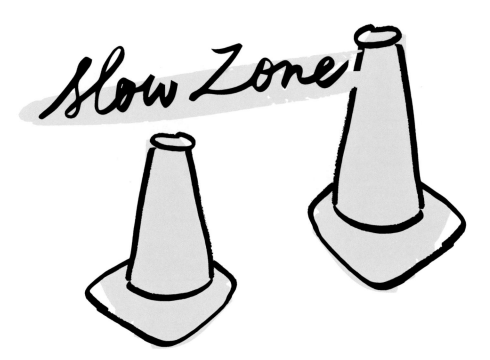

Silence And The Art Of Not Doing

Sometimes it pays to wait.

It has taken us years of practice to get good at sitting with silences in groups. Especially awkward silences where it feels like our clients are staring at us and willing us to do something.

But the more we practice sitting with silence, the more we find that what eventually happens—when someone in the group finally speaks—is nearly always way more interesting than anything we might have said to break the discomfort.
Letting the group live with a bit of quiet time can be very powerful. Time for thinking, catching one's breath, calming feelings, internal regrouping, and savoring success are some of the benefits.

Being silent is not the same as being absent. We are present to what is going on, we're managing the stream of thoughts in our head. We're reminding ourselves to breathe. It takes conscious effort to appear to do nothing. Inside our heads we have all sorts of ideas for what to do next in groups, and the art is to only act on a few of them.

shhh...

The Power Of Simple Social Contact

Whether it is online, or in-person, we need informal social contact.

Geoff Colvin* describes the continuing research done by a team at MIT, led by Alex Pentland. They are using tagging technology to analyse the frequency and nature of social contact between members of teams in many different locations. "(They) found that the best predictor of team productivity was how much the members interacted in a given period, and "engagement"—the degree to which all team members were involved in the interaction.

In-person social interaction helps the group elicit more ideas from all members and arrive at better judgments about those ideas. Together, face-to-face, we become literally smarter and more capable as a group than we ever could be when meeting virtually."

Perhaps the most headline-worthy finding is this: Pentland's team claims to be able to predict the creative quality of teams just by seeing the patterns of their connections, without analysing the content of their conversations at all. For those of us who believe facilitators need to focus more on process than content, this is an interesting bit of evidence

Although the research is based on in-person meetings, we think it has implications for how we meet, even when it's online.
We need to allow our online collaboration to encourage more informal conversations, not always driven by a fixed agenda.

* https://www.newsweek.com/creative-power-meeting-eyeball-eyeball-375666

Improv Principles

Being prepared to be spontaneous.

We need to be flexible and respond to what happens, moment-by-moment, in the room. It's easy to get attached to techniques and talk about 'trusting the process'— but it's vital to retain spontaneity and aliveness.

People have been to a lot of meetings and are rightly wary of being 'techniqued'. They need to see that the facilitator is awake to what's happening, and not just leading them to some pre-planned solutions. These are some of the ideas from improvised theatre that guide our work.

Accepting Offers is about seeing opportunities in what others say and do, rather than being defensive and blocking them. It doesn't mean you have to agree with them, but you can look for ways to acknowledge and build on what they bring. When dealing with complex and controversial topics, it helps to be able to include diverse perspectives and approaches.

Noticing more: When groups of people get stuck, it's easy to lose perspective and close down, missing a lot of what's going on. Anxiety tends to reduce our ability to see choices. By noticing more, we open ourselves up to new ways of responding. It counters the fight-or-flee instinct that can reduce our effectiveness under stress.

Let go: We remind ourselves to 'let go' often. What we need to let go of will vary. It might be our attachment to being right; it might be the way we've always done things; it might be our favourite activity. It's a reminder that it's easy to become rigid when flexibility is more useful.

Relax your clever: It's too easy to think we can manage complex people and situations by knowing better than other people. Expertise is fine, but if it stops us from spotting what is new by focussing only on what is familiar, it gets in everyone's way.

Be affected: Let what others do and say sink in and let it change you. People will notice and they'll understand that we have actually heard them.

Making your partner look good is about realising that the quality of your relationship will have more impact on others than the mere words you use. If you want playful collaboration, try to be an example of it.

Commit yourself: Sometimes when you're trying something new, it's easy to hedge your bets and be tentative. That's great up to a point, but groups will often respond cautiously if you don't commit yourself. By committing, you don't pretend to be infallible, but you do show that you really want to engage.

Move: When we say move, we're being deliberately ambiguous. We might mean move yourself, we might mean ask others to move. And we might mean physical movement, or emotional. It's easy to get stuck in a particular way of relating to people as if it's the obvious or only way to do it. It isn't.

There Is No Magic Formula, So Stop Looking

Every workshop is unique.

There is no magic formula for designing and conducting a workshop. There is no substitute for practice and experience. And then there's the paradox of facilitation: once you understand the theories and principles behind facilitation you then have to let them go. Think of something you do really well—it might be playing a musical instrument, drawing, driving a vehicle—and compare how you do that activity now compared to when you were first learning.

Facilitation is similar. While you are learning facilitation you will often want to refer to notes and guidelines and ideas from others, and as your skills and awareness and confidence grow, you will need to do this less often. So while you never stop learning about facilitation, there will come a time when you are able to confidently step into any facilitation role.

You can outline an approach and select activities to engage people. But the mark of a great facilitator is knowing that these are merely guidelines and will be jettisoned as soon as they are not useful or needed. Attentiveness and flexibility are key to good design and facilitation. Good facilitators frequently change what they've planned, on the spot (and on the fly), trusting their intuition—that's where their confidence comes from.

It's worth it to take time out to mull it over

Don't plan the workshop straight away. After your briefing, put all your notes aside and do something else. Leave it for a few days if you have the time. This gives your subconscious time to process what you have heard about the workshop. You will start to get ideas about what you could do.

Designing the workshop

This is where everyone wants a magic formula. There is none. Every workshop is different and should be designed as such. If you try to do the same thing each time, you'll end up, well, doing the same thing each time, which is not really serving the needs of the particular group.

Clients might expect that a facilitator can take a group on a complete journey, enabling the participants to return to their ordinary world of work, changed and with the answers to all their problems. The reality is quite different.

People sometimes get very animated about the need for completion and closure in meetings and this raises a red flag for us. It's often the unfinished work that means everyone has a reason to keep on working together after the event, continuing the journey.

You Wouldn't Paint By Numbers So Why Would You Facilitate By Numbers?

Facilitation insights from an art gallery.

There were 10 separate rooms at the Gauguin exhibition at the Tate Modern in London. Each room represented a different theme. It was very crowded. People shuffled around others to get closer to the pictures, stepped over pushers and avoided toes.

There were people of all ages, individually, sometimes in pairs or small groups, some well equipped, others with just a book and a pencil, copying Gauguin's work. Trish, our artist friend, explained that artists (like her) learn a lot from copying other artists. Especially great artists. Some like to copy the form—the strokes, the perspective, the composition. Trish gets inspiration from the use of colour. She might take just a few square centimetres of one of Gauguin's paintings and learn a lot about colour.

Who knew?

Which got us thinking about facilitation training—and, learning. We're always learning something new. This learning comes from many sources, some obvious, some downright weird. Watching, and being with, others. Reading. Playing improv games. Doing facilitation. Yes, that's right. Actually being a facilitator, and facilitating. And visiting art galleries.

It drives us nuts when facilitation is described mechanically: do this, then this, then that, and voila! Unfortunately, it never seems to quite work out that way in the real world.

So here's a paradox: we love helping others learn how to facilitate, work effectively with groups, upset entrenched patterns, surface emotions, unleash creativity, have big and small conversations. Yet, when someone asks us how we know to do this or that when facilitating, we're not sure. It's a bit like asking an artist how they knew to put that stroke exactly there, or why use those combinations of colours. Sometimes it just feels it right—through years and years of practice, through trial and error, through trusting ourselves. And by taking chances, being brave, being willing to make lots of mistakes before getting it 'right'. By mucking it up, throwing it out and starting over.

Knowing processes and activities is not enough. After learning all these techniques, budding facilitators come back to us and ask, "But how do you know which one to use?" "What's best?" "What should I do in such-and-such a situation?"

When is it okay to take away the master's painting and instead of copying someone else's work, begin with our own blank canvas? How do we learn to be comfortable with a blank canvas? You'll figure it out for yourself.

Beware The Tyrannies

Three traps to avoid.

One of the biggest barriers for facilitators using creative approaches is negative self talk, "I'm not creative". This is often expressed in what we call The Tyrannies.

The Tyrannies can show up for the group, and they can show up for the facilitator. It's wise to be ready.

The Tyranny of the Explicit: the fear of not knowing enough...

This is what happens when rules and procedures become counter productive. By trying to get everything written down, we think we're creating more certainty and safety, but risk losing the flexibility that makes us human. Adding rules tends to reduce exceptions, which can eliminate error, but also reduces innovation and starts to undermine motivation.

The Tyranny of Excellence: the fear of not being good enough...

This is where the perfect becomes the enemy of the good. The risk is that we set impossible standards and then get demoralised by not reaching them. The demand for perfection makes us hyper-critical and we fail to appreciate what we are actually achieving. When we lose that sense of reality, ironocally, we're more likely to fail or perhaps to give up altogether.

The Tyranny of Effort: the fear of not trying hard enough...

We act as if by just doing what we're doing with more intensity, we'll get a better result. Occasionally, trying harder can be just the thing - but more often it leaves us noticing less and getting increasingly stuck. We're doing more of what is already not working, and it becomes a form of punishment. Sometimes we visit the tyranny on ourselves and sometimes on others.

We call these tyrannies, because like any tyranny, they oppress us and limit our capacity to perform.

Escape The Plenary Vortex

Stop people either hogging the time, or disengaging completely.

Once you get more than around five people in a meeting it easily slides into a discussion that appears animated and productive, but the quality of engagement really suffers. With too many people, everyone's natural wish to speak means there is a scarcity of time. So you get more interruptions and a general spirit of competition for airtime. Even if things are polite on the surface, a sense of conflict becomes almost inevitable. People talk faster because they fear being cut off, and people stop listening carefully as they try to crowbar their way in. They're either talking, or reloading. Some people are more effective at getting heard, and others clam up.

You end up with a small number of louder participants having a conversation just with each other. Everyone else just gets to watch.

When people don't speak much, not only do we miss what they have to say, but they also miss the chance to think differently by speaking. We often don't realise that speaking is not only about explaining things to others, it's actually an important form of thinking. So unwieldy plenaries can be incredibly wasteful.

There's much to be said for breaking into smaller groups.

It is possible to have great plenary sessions but we need to do so quite carefully, with more sensitivity to the pitfalls of the vortex. That means including more reflective processes and a different sense of the kinds of conversation we can hold, encouraging a less linear way of listening to the ideas being shared—where we consciously listen for variety and not getting trigger happy in our responses. Sometimes you have to discourage the louder voices from speaking and wait for more reflective types to join the conversation.

The Value Of Unsafe Thinking

When ideas come up that make people anxious, let's see if we can make it safe to explore further, rather than closing discussion down.

Jonah Sachs is the author of *Unsafe Thinking*. He looks at people and organisations that have found success by being willing to explore apparently risky ideas.

He says that when confronted with anxiety, most of us stick to what we know and this prevents us seeing new possibilities. Instead he suggests moving towards anxiety. That doesn't mean taking reckless action, but rather pausing to look more carefully at the things we fear doing.

He uses the example of the US chain store, CVS pharmacy. It was generating $2bn in tobacco sales. An executive suggested abandoning those sales as inconsistent with the positioning of CVS in health. Most of her colleagues pushed back: those $2bn couldn't be jeopardised. But she went away and did some research and was able to suggest that the eventual effect would be positive. The store made the change and saw a huge increase in business.

Sachs warns of the danger of getting into expert mode, where we become defensive on subjects where we know a lot. This can blind us to changes that make our expertise more questionable.

Sachs suggests the practice of doing things you are not good at to keep alert. Viv recently had a go at stand up comedy in this spirit.

He also talks about the benefits of open mode: slowing down enough to reflect more carefully about the problems we're addressing. By slowing down, we make it easier to think riskier thoughts and have a more measured way of assessing their potential impact.

He uses the example of a basketball coach whose philosophy was to make the locker room a safe space, eschewing shouting and attacking, with the principle that this would allow the team to take more risks on court.

None of these principles, of course, will guarantee success in an uncertain world, but we think they are good ideas for facilitators to reflect on.

The Wisdom Of Uncertainty

It's easy to create big goals and detailed to-do lists. But in doing so, we often set ourselves up for failure.

In her blog post Stop Overplanning, Maria Popova explores* the wisdom of uncertainty.

"Indeed, of all the disappointments in life, there is hardly a kind more hazardous to happiness and more toxic to the soul than disappointing ourselves as we fail to live up to our own ideals and expectations."

We attempt to meet present-moment discontent with bold plans for the future. This appears to manage away our uncertainty, but sets us up with goals that often distract us from the creative potential of the moment. Popova quotes author Oliver Burkeman:

"Faced with the anxiety of not knowing what the future holds, we invest ever more fiercely in our preferred vision of that future—not because it will help us achieve it, but because it helps rid us of feelings of uncertainty in the present."

Burkeman goes on to challenge the idea that great inventors and entrepreneurs are guided by a driving vision. Instead, he presents research suggesting the opposite:

"The most valuable skill of a successful entrepreneur ... isn't "vision" or "passion" or a steadfast insistence on destroying every barrier between yourself and some prize you're obsessed with. Rather, it's the ability to adopt an unconventional approach to learning: an improvisational flexibility not merely about which route to take towards some predetermined objective, but also a willingness to change the destination itself."

One of the most satisfying practices of facilitation is to resist the urge to fix uncomfortable situations with a process or a solution. Often, if we simply slow down and accept unexpected surprises and pitfalls, the group itself will generate more creative ideas and solutions than we would have rushed to. As facilitators, we often feel impulses to do things, and then choose not act on them.

When there's a long silence, rather than fill it with a clever question or rush to a break, sit a bit longer and see what happens. When someone interrupts us and we feel like offering a quick fire response to move them on, what if we relax and say, "Tell us more?". When a group descends into apparent confusion, what if we don't rush to help but relax and see if they can figure it out for themselves?

Each time we follow this principle, we have to sit with our uncertainties. We tolerate our fear that people will think we're incompetent or don't care. We live with the anxiety that something might go wrong if we don't act. We find there are often big rewards for this approach—but it takes practice.

* https://www.brainpickings.org/2014/02/05/oliver-burkeman-antidote-plans-uncertainty/

Avoid Creeping Death

Avoid the tedium of conventional reporting back.

You have a large group working on important issues. Naturally, at some time during the workshop there will be small group work, and you will be tempted to have a reporting back session to the whole group. The reporting back may even take longer than the initial small group discussions. Please try to think of another way. We've done it ourselves when lost for ideas and regretted it. Reporting back is nearly always tedious and energy-sapping.

The whole small group scribing-reporting back scenario is based on some educational echo of the teacher making sure you've been doing the task as instructed and some checking that you 'got it'. Problem is, we are not at school, we are not children, there probably is no 'right' answer, and the facilitator's role is not to check-up on the quality of the work.

The purpose of small group work is to enable greater engagement with a topic, to enable more voices to be heard, to have deeper, more meaningful conversations. Keeping notes of the conversation and reporting back may not add additional value, and may even detract.

We sometimes skip reporting back altogether. We know that if something really important happens in a breakout group, people will find a way to bring it back to the room. Or we might use a process in which everyone can post their own feedback to questions posted around the room *(see our online notes on Full Circle: https://www.creativefacilitation.com/s/Full-Circle.pdf)*

The Teaching Trance

By avoiding the trappings of expertise, we become more vulnerable but create more power and agency for the group.

It's easy to slip into a teaching trance. You can end up doing it as a facilitator, or you can allow groups to slide into it if certain voices come to dominate the meeting.

On the surface, it looks like serious engagement is happening as a speaker dispenses knowledge and the participants appear to be respectfully appreciating it. This can be flattering to the ego of the speaker, and quite comforting to the audience, reducing their responsibility for the learning. The speaker gets repeated signals that she's supposed to be authoritative, and becomes quite attached to the power and/or responsibility.

In the teaching trance, we all become attached to explanation and answers, and the surprise of discovery becomes a threat.

But discovery is what really imprints learning. As David Rock and Jeffrey Schwartz say in their article, The Neuroscience of Leadership*: *"For insights to be useful, they need to be generated from within, not given to individuals as conclusions…. Human brains are so complex and individual that there is little point in trying to work out how another person ought to reorganize his or her thinking. It is far more effective and efficient to help others come to their own insights."*

* https://www.strategy-business.com/article/06207?gko=f1af3

The Value Of Loose Ends

Sometimes unfinished business is a great way to keep people engaged.

In Monty Python's Life of Brian, the eponymous antihero is fleeing a brigade of Roman soldiers. In his panic, he falls from a ledge into a spot where a variety of zany religious types are preaching to would-be followers. Brian nervously delivers a sermon in the hope of blending into the background and eluding his pursuers.

He's not very good. The crowd challenges the details of his story, and the more stressed he becomes, the less convincing is his performance. Fortunately, the soldiers pass by and he can relax. So he abandons his story mid-sentence. It doesn't really matter anymore.

But this is just the point at which the audience moves from scepticism to curiosity. The unfinished nature of the story hooks them. As a result, a massive crowd builds up, trying to make sense of what's happening, pursuing all manner of hilarious misunderstandings.

Sometimes it's better to leave people curious enough to start to generate their own meanings and answers, instead of spoon feeding. Several times in this book, we've resisted the urge to spell out solutions to some of the challenges and dilemmas we've described. We're trusting your capacity to work some things out for yourself.

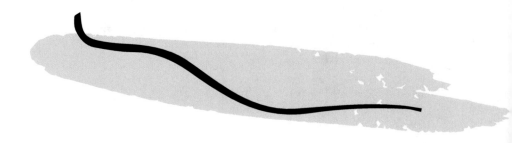

Premature encapsulation.

We sometimes use the phrase "premature encapsulation" to describe trying to tie the results of a meeting up in a pretty bow. We anxiously try to convince ourselves that something useful happened—an artificial summarising and committing to next steps or action before people are ready.

When do we really know that something is finished?

And why is finishing so important? Maybe early Hollywood movies and television sit-coms are to blame. There's an expectation that all the loose ends will be neatly tied up by the end. If you expect the same in facilitated workshops you will work towards achieving that, increasing the chances of missing something else that is important.

Why unfinished business may be even better than finishing.

The Zeigarnik effect says that people remember incomplete or interrupted tasks better than completed ones. This raises interesting questions about not finishing, about providing more space for relationship building and the amount of time people need in workshop to do certain tasks, as well as motivating people to continue to follow up/follow through on new actions, approaches, processes.

Nothing Is Written

Life is unruly and unpredictable - our best approach is to remain open, curious and flexible. Rather than giving people reassuring "right answers" we may do better to model experimentation, curiosity and openness.

In the film Lawrence of Arabia, there's a scene where Lawrence is crossing the desert. One of his group, Gasim, has fallen from his camel and is lost. The tribesmen tell Lawrence that to return for him would lead to certain death under the unforgiving sun—"it is written".

It's a common human response to stress. Rather than admit to anxiety or doubt, we double down on vehemently held beliefs. We seek to tame the unknown and the complex by eliminating any talk of risk or possibility. We feel safer talking about the state of the world than admitting a humbler truth about our fears and uncertainties.

Rather than admit to sadness for Gasim, or fear for themselves, they talk about "the way things are". In so many work situations, people would rather say "that won't work" or "this is how we've always done it" than admit "I don't know".

Unwilling to leave Gasim to die, Lawrence defies this wisdom and vanishes into the sands in search of him. He subsequently returns, with Gasim alive, and tells the bedouin, "nothing is written".

Shared Peril

There is nothing like the connection people can make by experimenting and discovering together. If you serve people the answers, you take away the possibility of shared discovery.

Few things can bond a group of people like shared peril. If the group comes together in the face of adversity, its sense of camaraderie and trust increases. Without the element of shared peril, these moments of growth would not happen.

Of course, adversity can also break a group. So the focus must be on allowing participants to manage their own experience, so they can be on the edge of their comfort zone, and not pushed beyond it.

And the facilitator must be willing to share in the experience. If we only create peril for the participants, that's more a kind of bullying than learning. We should drop our masks of expertise and reveal our vulnerability.

Beware Of Commitment Ceremonies

Beware of half-hearted action planning.

Nowadays, as workshops near a close, there's often pressure for some process that gets people to agree on what actions need to happen and who's going to be responsible for them. There's a certain amount of anxiety attached to this, often to do with having something to present to powers-that-be outside the room, to prove that the event hasn't just been a talking-shop. And it certainly conforms to a neat and tidy notion of meetings following a linear path that ends in certainty and completion.

The trouble is, in the real world, these action planning sessions often feel pretty deadly and inauthentic. They tend to assume that action is what is needed now, as opposed to say further reflection; the people in the room are uniquely empowered to act, when frequently they aren't; and everyone's nicely aligned and all are agreed on what should happen.

Often, people will go along with these commitment ceremonies not because they're wildly enthused but because saying "yes" now means the ordeal will end soon. They know how these things work: what's agreed here may have only a passing resemblance to what will actually happen in the real world anyway.

What you can end up with is pseudo-agreements that mean boxes get ticked for productivity, but it's not very convincing. On the upside, it can be quite polite and conflicts may, sometimes, be avoided—for now.

Of course, sometimes there is lots of agreement and a well-focused exercise in coordinating future actions is just the thing. But often this is just done ritualistically.

Here's what we tend to find more satisfying in a lot of contexts: instead of focusing on actions, we try to get groups to be clear about what point they have reached, in a way that means every-one speaks and gets heard. So we might have a round where everyone gets a chance to check in, perhaps responding to a very open question that lets them choose to report what they've learnt, what they are concerned about, what they see happening next... without a sense that only "action" is to be the focus.

What often happens is that the group gets a few surprises in this process, realising that a lot has been going on for people and that people in the room are often responding in quite different ways: some are reflective, some inspired, some anxious. Quite often, it turns out the people have already agreed on actions anyway, and these are much more convincing than those you get from an action ritual.

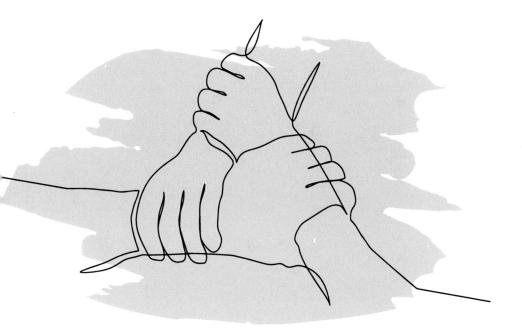

Step Away From The Flipchart!

Don't spend much time at flipcharts writing things.

We don't like making ourselves the centre of attention, and we don't think it's our job to record the work of the group.

Not everything has to be recorded. Being in a conversation, throwing around ideas, challenging each other, hearing diverse points of view—this is the work of a workshop. The human brain will process all of this over time and whatever is important will be retained. It's a false insurance to think that everything that is important needs to be written down or recorded, or that everything that is written or recorded is important.

Who benefits from workshop notes being typed into a report?
What usually happens is *more reports sitting on shelves (or on computers)*.

Instead, capture the information as part of the workshop process. It is far more useful to encourage those responsible for using what emerges to capture it, than for the facilitator to prepare a report that no-one reads. Sometimes a workshop report is included as part of an organisation's contract when engaging a facilitator. Check what this means, how it will be used, and who will use it. This information will help determine the type of report, if any, is actually needed. And, which group members might still be the best choice for capturing relevant sections. This will also keep group members feeling a part of the process and reinforces their responsibility for the outcomes.

In some cases you might want to keep your own process notes. Process notes can be a helpful reminder for debriefing, learning and understanding the difference between what you actually did and what you planned to do. This is quite different from content notes.

Let The Group Do The Work

The number one thing we share on our facilitation training.

Are you being run off your feet? Are you trying to capture every comment during a discussion? Are you up the front of the room, on your feet, working hard while the participants are sitting? You're working too hard!

Take a short break and explore how you can get the participants to do the work. There's many benefits to this: they will become more involved and contribute, you will have time and space to think about and prepare for what's next, and will have more "pride of ownership" of ideas and outcomes, which increases the likelihood of their continuing commitment after the workshop is over. They will do a better job than you anyway and you will be able to focus more on group dynamics.

Doing the work on behalf of the group is not helping the group. This is an easy mistake to make. Whether it be to prove their worth to the group, or to demonstrate their knowledge of the topic, or simply because that's what they have seen others do, doing the work on behalf of the group may feel good in the short term but rarely pays off. Participants can disengage, the work will probably go nowhere as there's little or no ownership. You won't be there afterwards, and even if you are, you will have your own work to deal with. If you are a part of the group, you may even feel a little miffed, even a bit resentful, that they let you do all the work. That's not a good place to be.

The role of the facilitator is to enable and motivate the group to do their own work.

Process, Schmocess

The process is the least important thing: what matters is the people who are using it.

We are often asked how we know which is the best activity to use, but we're wary of suggesting there's a right process for any situation.

Having a number of activities to draw on is useful. What is even more useful though is being present to what is happening in the group and asking yourself, in the moment, what could I do now? Sometimes the answer might be to just get out of the way, other times it might be to use one of these activities. The only way to know what to use, when, is to be familiar with them by using them. We think the real skill of facilitation is not an encyclopaedic knowledge of tips, tricks and games to play with people, but an awareness of when, and how, to nudge people in a particular direction - to sense when they need a change of pace, a change of scenery, or a change of focus.

We don't use the facilitator's standard catchphrase of "trust the process." When Johnnie did his psychotherapy training, the trainers would refuse, in their phrase, to give out recipe cards. Human relationships can't be operated like a machine, according to some simple (or worse, complicated) formula.

They instead emphasised the value of being present to the relationships, paying attention to our own and others' feelings and responses. The most powerful intervention might be simply to acknowledge what's happening. The simple statement, "I noticed you sighing as you said that," might unleash a tide of feeling and information that the clumsy implementation of a process would have missed.

The 'Sitcom' Syndrome

A maths guru teaches us "patient problem solving".

Many of us used to like maths, the problem solving and the patterns—until we got a teacher who sucked all the enthusiasm out of it.

Dan Meyer is an American maths advocate. He used to teach high school maths to students who didn't like high school maths. He sparked my theory about some workshops wanting to be like sitcoms by describing an 'impatience with irresolution' where we come to expect a sitcom-style 22 minute resolution to all of our problems.

He advocates 'patient problem solving' and suggests that a teacher's role is to use compelling questions and student intuition to arrive at compelling answers. He argues that existing maths text books provide a smooth, or easy, route, whereas patient problem solving involves conversation.

Hmmm, this all sounds very familiar.

> **Meyer suggests five steps to better maths engagement:**
>
> 1. **Use multimedia**
> 2. **Encourage intuition**
> 3. **Ask the shortest question you can**
> 4. **Let (participants) build the problem**
> 5. **Be less helpful**

Could just as easily be applied to facilitation. The problem with many workshops is that there is an expectation that whatever problem or issue has been brewing for the last few weeks, months, or even years, will be resolved by the end of a workshop.

There might be some agreement, but people return to their desks the next day and reset back to where they began, just like a sitcom. There's no change, growth, or development.

Don't Get Mired In Information

Stop information dumps from killing the energy of your meeting.

"Information is a very weak form of communication" — Viola Spolin

We're not fans of "one-to-many" processes. A one-to-many process is one person doing something while everyone else is not doing much at all. A presentation is a good example. The argument goes like this: there's 'certain' information that everyone needs to know before they can proceed. The 'best' way to make sure everyone has this information is to do a presentation.

This assumes that giving information and knowing is the same thing. Some information is shared so poorly, we know that most people have mentally switched off and taken in little or nothing of what was said. How can this be a good use of time together?

Great presentations do enable people to engage with the speaker's message, to recall what it was and to be moved to some action as a result. When was the last time you attended a great presentation in your organisation?

Many meetings default to sharing information or rely on the presenter-audience format. Often it's too hard to do anything else. The world is complex, and multi-layered and the work people are doing can be much the same. The pace of change and development in most fields is so fast it's hard, if not impossible, to keep up-to-date.

For many people, the presenter-audience format is the only way they know how to meet. They haven't experienced other approaches to meetings, approaches that involve everyone, that draw out their knowledge and ideas; that generate enthusiasm and shared learning. All meetings, gatherings, events, and conferences, can be energised this way and made more meaningful and memorable for all participants.

Here are some ways to breakdown the monotony of the one-to-many format.

POPCORN POWERPOINT

Prepare 30-50 slides. Each slide should represent a specific, single message about the topic and be designed using bold images, colours and minimal text. Number each of the slides.

Tell the audience that you have 50 slides on the topic, but they will decide which slides you will talk about – and they will only choose five of the 50 slides.

Ask for a random number between 1 and 50. Go to that slide and talk about it. Then ask for another number.

Repeat.

Can also ask the audience to comment on the slides, or to tell their own stories about the slide.

FROM PRESENTATION TO CONVERSATION

Suppose you've got four 20 minute presentations that your client insists must be given to a roomful of people. Instead of sitting as a huge, static audience for 80 minutes, you could ask the four presenters to go the corners of the room. Split the audience into four groups to spend 20 minutes with each speaker. Run four rounds, with the groups moving from speaker-to-speaker. Each speaker gets to work with smaller groups - much more comfortable and conversational, and gets to practice their pitch four times, learning as they go. And everyone else gets to engage in a smaller group, and to get some movement into their legs.

CREATING BETTER PRESENTATIONS, IF YOU MUST

Powerpoint presentations, along with email, have become the default way of communicating in many organisations. The main problem with slideshows is that the presenter uses the tool (Powerpoint) the wrong way. Here's what typically happens. You've been asked to give a talk. You have a 20 minute slot in a jam-packed program. You sit down at your computer and start planning your talk. You use the Powerpoint slides to do this. Filling in details as you go, listing all the things you want to say. You find a few photographs to break up the text and insert those. You even find a cool quote and add that. You've heard about slide sorter, so you use that to rearrange your slides. You make sure the company logo is on every slide (maybe your organisation even provides a template for your slideshow). You do one more run through, and you're done. Sound familiar?

We can't begin to tell you how wrong this is—what a waste of time it is, for you, and ultimately your audience. It might be useful to think about your slideshow in four parts:

1. Message: What is the key message you are trying to leave with your audience?

2. Slides: These support what you are saying by reinforcing the message or providing visuals to drive home a point

3. Your notes: Where you write all the things you want to say (these can either accompany each slide, or be on cards, but are not visible to the audience)

4. Handout: Yes that's right, a handout that includes all the additional data that supports your argument or idea, such as graphs and tables and extra information. It is not a copy of your slides and best not to distribute it before your talk.

Movement And Play

Our bodies are designed to move, our minds are designed to learn from play.

We are often asked how we know which is the best activity to use, but we're wary. There are many reasons for playing games in workshops, and we often use them to surface particular behaviours or thinking, or as a platform to explore a particular topic.

And sometimes we just play games for fun. Playing a game just for fun uses different parts of the brain and creates new neural connections. After a period of play, participants often quickly resolve issues they were struggling with, see things differently, or have new insights.

Sitting, thinking, even engaging in lively conversation, can become tiring after a few hours. Try and encourage your participants to engage their whole body during a workshop, not just the part above the neck. That means moving. Standing up, sitting down, moving across the room, making choices, walking and talking. Plan for, and encourage, as much movement as possible.

Who Is Viola Spolin?

She is one of our biggest influences, and a pioneer of improv theatre.

One of our influences is the American improvisation guru, Viola Spolin. She grew up with a fierce interest in games and went on to do inspiring work using drama to work with children. Her cardinal principle was not to teach children things like stagecraft, but to turn it into a game from which they could make discoveries of their own.

One example is her invention of the game "stage picture". She noticed that her actors would struggle with creating good sightlines for the audience when on stage - they would stand so that they blocked the audience's view of key performers. So Spolin invented "Stage Picture". In this game, whenever she called out, "Stage picture", the children had to instantly move to a position where people in the theatre seats could have a clear line of sight to them. By playing the game, the actors learned to stay in sight. No lecture or admonishment needed.

It's a great inspiration to us to be playful and experimental, and to focus on creating experiences for participants rather than talking at them. Spolin's approach encourages us to play another game and to look at ways games can help us solve a problem with a problem.

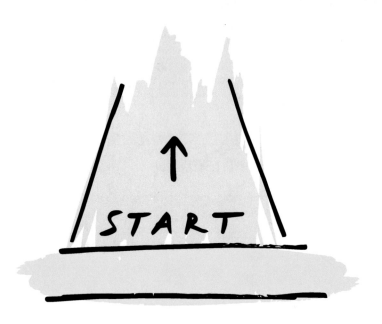

Start Before You're Ready

Humans are quite talented at overthinking.

Some challenges are better dealt with by experimenting and allowing for mistakes. It's often better than analysis paralysis.

We notice this most often when briefing our activities to groups. It's why we tend to give shorter explanations and get people started sooner. We tend not to ask for questions. One of our favourite things is to say instead, raise your hand if you've got enough information to start work? Usually, most people raise their hands. Then we say, great, that's enough to start. And if you haven't got your hand up, talk to someone who has, or come and chat to us. (If you start taking questions, you can spend ages worrying about hypothetical issues and slip into what we call a plenary vortex - described earlier in this book.)

Neglect The Space At Your Peril

Setting the room sets the mood for the meeting.

We think the space you work in is important, and one of the most neglected aspects of facilitation. The space people walk into sends an immediate message about the type of event this will be.

Often, a client will choose the space for a workshop not knowing that some spaces work better than others. We've had to work in board rooms with immovable tables, art galleries where nothing can be posted on the walls, in restaurants where there's no room to move. We try and make the best use of these spaces, or move outside or somewhere else.

In our ideal world the best spaces are about twice the size that the group actually needs, with plenty of wall and floor space, no tables, natural light, and access to the outdoors.

The Hitchhiker's Guide To Facilitation

Brilliant insights for meetings from a master of science fiction.

by Andrew Rixon

Inspired by a reference to Douglas Adams' Hitchhikers Guide to the Galaxy 5, I thought it could be a bit of fun to take a look at three phrases that are found within and see how they might provide some insight into facilitating better meetings. After all, not unlike a group facilitator, being a galactic hitchhiker will see you needing to be crafty, resourceful, nimble and travelling light!

The Answer's 42

In the first novel and radio series, a group of hyper-intelligent pan-dimensional beings demand to learn the Ultimate Answer to the Ultimate Question of Life, The Universe, and Everything from the super-computer, Deep Thought, specially built for this purpose. It takes Deep Thought 7½ million years to compute and check the answer, which turns out to be 42. Unfortunately, The Ultimate Question itself is unknown.

How often have you been in a meeting where people are focusing on jumping to answers, regardless of what the problem or question actually is? It's interesting to notice how quickly people sometimes want to jump into action, but at the cost of not laying the groundwork for what's needed in making these actions sustainable. Like, for instance, building relationships.

Thinking there's one right answer and it's 42 is a whole other problem for meetings. This manifests itself by way of pre-determined outcomes and an inability to accept emergent outcomes.

This leads us naturally on to the next principle.

2 DON'T PANIC

In the series, DON'T PANIC (always upper-case) is a phrase written on the cover of The Hitchhiker's Guide to the Galaxy. The novel explains that this was partly because the device "looked insanely complicated" to operate, and partly to keep inter-galactic travelers from panicking. It is said that despite its many glaring (and occasionally fatal) inaccuracies, the Hitchhiker's Guide to the Galaxy itself has outsold the Encyclopedia Galactica because it is slightly cheaper, and because it has the words "Don't Panic" in large, friendly letters on the cover. Arthur C. Clarke said Douglas Adams' use of "don't panic" was perhaps the best advice that could be given to humanity.

I remember a session at the Australian Facilitators' Conference several years ago titled "Don't freak out—Doing your best facilitation". With the wisdom of moving beyond "the answer is 42", come the hair-raising truth of getting to know all about emergent outcomes, first hand. Not to mention experiencing the emotions and reactions of groups working their way through difficult situations.

It's deceptively simple: "don't panic" means breathe... In... breathe... Out...

3 Knowing where one's towel is

Somebody who can stay in control of virtually any situation is somebody who "knows where his or her towel is". The logic behind this statement is presented in Chapter 3 of The Hitchhiker's Guide to the Galaxy thus:

"....a towel has immense psychological value. For some reason, if a strag (strag: nonhitchhiker) discovers that a hitchhiker has his towel with him, he will automatically assume that he is also in possession of a toothbrush, washcloth, soap, tin of biscuits, flask, compass, map, ball of string, gnat spray, wet-weather gear, space suit etc., etc. Furthermore, the strag will then happily lend the hitchhiker any of these or a dozen other items that the hitchhiker might accidentally have "lost". What the strag will think is that any man who can hitch the length and breadth of the galaxy, rough it, slum it, struggle against terrible odds, win through, and still knows where his towel is, is clearly a man to be reckoned with."

Personally, for a group facilitator, I think knowing where one's towel is, is about knowing the purpose for bringing the group together. Understanding at a deep level what the meeting is really about. All the other things (processes, flipcharts, marker pens and sticky dots) are like the hitchhiker's toothbrush, washcloth, soap and biscuits. Understanding the purpose and what is bringing the group together will, like the towel, provide immense psychological value; further helping you with the previous principle "Don't panic".

Get Rid Of The Tables

All of them. Here's why.

1. It's too easy to set up 'camp' at a table

Notebook here. Pen there. Glass, coffee cup, cell phone, laptop. Coat over the back of the chair. Once settled, imagine how hard it's going to be to get that person to move all their goods and chattels? While it's possible to 'set up camp' around a chair, it has a less permanent feel. And why is 'setting up camp' a bad thing? Because the focus is on things, not people. And if it's one of my workshops, I'm going to ask you to move around. I'd rather you be less encumbered with physical stuff as I have enough trouble dealing with the mental stuff you're probably also carrying around. Also, by removing the "ordinary", we are encouraging fresh thinking and new ideas.

2. Tables get in the way

Somewhere there's a guidebook that conference centres use. I'm sure it tells them the minimum amount of space required for a group of any size. So if you call a venue to book a room and say you have 30 people, they will squeeze your group into a room that is okay for 30 people as long as they just want to sit and do nothing but listen. These small rooms become manageable when the tables are removed. It's then possible to use all the space, and to reconfigure the group into whatever group sizes work for the purpose of the meeting.

3. Tables get in the way II

Tables keep people apart. They get in the way of activities. They get in the way of the facilitator entering the group. They define differences: what is the group space and what is the facilitator space. The worst sort of tables are those large round banquet tables. Even with only a few people at each table, they tend to en-courage talking with your immediate neighbour and inhibit talking with those way across the table.

4. Tables have echoes of classrooms

A workshop, a training, a meeting can be stressful for all concerned. And if your memories of classrooms at school are unhappy, then even in a different setting, a different configuration—tables have echoes of class-rooms and the same old defensiveness may surface for some participants.

5. Tables pre-determine the front of the room

If you have a rectangular room, the front will nearly always be at the narrow end. This is based on the assumption of a speaker and passive listeners, and fitting in the maximum number of people. This can be a problem if the room is particularly long - it's hard to maintain eye contact and build rapport with those at the back of the room. Flip it around and have the front of the room along the long edge and everyone feels closer. Much easier to do this if there's no tables already in place.

Common objections to removing the tables

Where do I put my stuff?
It's not business-as-usual, so leave your stuff at your desk. And if you still have stuff, how about stashing it under your chair? And if it is business-as-usual, why are you having a meeting in the first place?

It's too hard to take notes
Carry a small notebook, maybe one without lines, one that fits into a pocket and a pen. Anything really important can be provided by the person organising the meeting. No need to split your attention between taking notes and participating.

The tables are permanent/too hard to move/there's no-where to put the tables (and similar variations)

Too easy. Find a new space.

Status Games

Changing your status - by words or actions - can unlock all sorts of challenges.

Status is something we've learned from improv theatre. It's about how you behave towards others, and is sometimes referred to as dominant and submissive behaviours.

Status, or power games, are inherent in meetings and workshops - whether acknowledged or not. Sometimes status can get in the way, creating tension between individuals and limiting the potential for authentic communication and engagement. Status plays out in many ways: sometimes a connection occurs between strangers and they just feel they communicate on the same wave-length; or a careless step on someone's toes (an unseen status challenge) creates tension between individuals. A facilitator is in a unique status position and has an advantage to see status gaps, and disrupt status games. We can't avoid status games. They are part of human dynamics and relationships. We can learn to recognize the impact of status and how to effectively respond.

Keith Johnstone, a pioneer of improv theatre, told a great story about three kinds of teachers: *"There was the teacher we liked but who couldn't keep discipline; another teacher who was generally disliked—never punished, yet exerted a ruthless discipline. A third teacher, who was much loved, never punished but kept excellent discipline, while remaining very human...The incompetent teacher was a low-status player: he twitched, he made many unnecessary movements, he went red at the slightest annoyance, and he always seemed like an intruder in the classroom. The one who filled us with terror was a compulsive high-status player. The third was a status expert, raising and lowering his status with great skill."*

Status is something you choose to express—not the endowed status you carry because of your position or title or background (although these obviously play out as well). Understanding the dynamics of status is a brilliant tool for facilitators. Not only does it provide a lens in which to view the sometimes baffling behaviour of participants, it is also a way of using your own status, that is raising or lowering it, to influence the group's behaviour. Status is the tool we already use to create distance or closeness between people.

Whether we are aware or not, we embody and play out status games in facilitation. There are multiple interventions drawn from improvisational theatre that disrupt entrenched behaviours and patterns of status.

Changing status can sometimes affect how we feel and how the group feels. Essentially, we can vary our status from low to high, often unconsciously. Sometimes if we get stuck in high status—for example, standing up when the group is sitting, or taking charge of the flip chart, or shouting—the group starts to react against it, raising stress. Equally, if we get stuck in low status (shuffling, avoiding eye contact for example), the group may not take us seriously. It's helpful to be able to shift your status. Be aware of your approach, and your status throughout an engagement and how it is affecting individual participants and the group as a whole.

Stories Connect

Our stories connect us in a way that information doesn't. Yet we sometimes think that storytelling is child's play, not serious work.

There are many types of story work, and when people hear the word story they sometimes think of made-up or fairy stories. While these can and do have applications in facilitation, more often we'll be using people's own stories of their experiences.

These stories can help people connect with each other by providing a bridge between diverse, yet ultimately human, experiences, and may reveal underlying themes or surface questions that can be explored. We use stories to unearth ideas and understanding that emerge from your own personal experience.

If people have trouble finding their stories it can be helpful to use pictures or found objects to spark a memory, or to start with something simple like a story about arriving at the workshop.

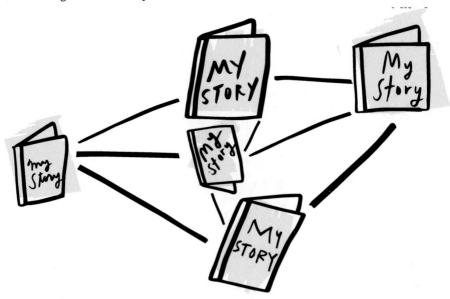

Finish On Time

The challenge posed by 'not enough time' can be a useful way to push people beyond their comfort zone.

We don't care what time the workshop starts (well, actually we do—we'd prefer it started dead on time, every time, but...sigh...it rarely does) but it's really important to finish on time or earlier.

Finishing on time honours the people in the room, not just their comments and their expertise, but also their time and that they have lives beyond the workshop. Finishing on time sends a message that we value their input during the workshop and we value them as people too. And we've also made a contract with the participants to start on time and finish on time. The very least we can do is honour our side of the bargain.

Shorten breaks, drop activities, do whatever it takes to finish on time. The key is to adapt throughout the workshop and especially during the last hours. Working backwards helps. We might have up to half a dozen timing plans in our heads during the last part of a workshop to make sure we finish right on time. Because we know what else needs to be done, and about how long it will take, if we need to stop something or someone from going on and on, we will.

The role of a facilitator is to challenge, disrupt, and encourage participants to do the work they need to do in whatever time is available, not necessarily in whatever time is ideal.

Facilitating Online

Virtual meetings magnify facilitation pitfalls

Facilitating online is more challenging because participants are often more easily distracted, and the technology itself can easily become tiring.

Many of the challenges we talk about in this book are amplified online. The plenary vortex gets worse. For example, someone asks a question. The facilitator answers. A conversation develops between the questioner and the facilitator, while everyone else observes with increasing boredom or simply gets on with their email.

Another feature of online is that the facilitator is easily kept stimulated - they have even more to manage than in a regular meeting - but they don't realise that what is highly engaging - even if stressful - for them is often really unsatisfying for anyone else to observe. As you frantically fiddle with Zoom breakouts, everyone else is just kept waiting.

A busy facilitator, entranced by their screens, can fall even deeper into a teaching trance. A good online meeting is not one person explaining things. Our principle of not bombarding people with data applies even more strongly online.

High tech, high touch
You may be using clever technology, but the most valuable resource is human intelligence. Don't get people mesmerised by fiddling with screens and keyboards. Cluttered "whiteboards" often create the sizzle of participation but can be noisy and confusing. Allow your meetings to have visceral life, with movement, surprise and emotion.

The job of the facilitator is to bring even more humanity and creativity to the work, not to get mired in the latest technological tricks. Make the most of your human voice — warm, vulnerable and open - instead of getting stuck in impersonal webcast mode.

Step away from the camera: you don't need to make people spend the whole meeting staring at their screen. Create a reflective activity they can do away from their computer, perhaps using pen and paper to create a different state. Have them find an object in their workspace and use it as a prompt for sharing something about themselves. Create exercises for people to stand and move in and out of screen according to their answer to a question. Maybe get people to wave hands and gesticulate strongly to take their turn in a meeting, it gets them more physically active.

Use the technology playfully. You can sometimes get people to turn cameras off to change the feeling of the meeting and focus on the voices rather than the standard screens. Use features on Zoom like "hide non-video participants" to allow some of the conversation to focus on a few people and give others a rest.

1 Breakout or die
Smaller breakouts - and lots of them - will do wonders for energy levels. It shifts the focus and breaks the trance of the screen.

2 Get a co-facilitator
Online facilitation is more demanding because of the need to manage the technology - and all the things that can go wrong with it. Having a co-facilitator is almost essential.

3 Put more love into offline materials
There's only so much you can do with a group online before fatigue sets in - for the participants and the facilitators - especially given what else is going on in the world, our communities, and our families. Because you can't risk over-loading your online meetings, you need to get creative and caring about the content you share before and after the meeting.

If your documents aren't clear, you end up wasting valuable meeting time explaining. That time could be used much more creatively by your participants. What you send out needs to be appealing and engaging.

About Creative Facilitation

Creative Facilitation was founded by Johnnie Moore, UK, and Viv McWaters, Australia. We support change and innovation in organisations by hosting better meetings and supporting more effective conversations.

We use a wide range of processes, including many we've invented ourselves, to help groups get the most out of their time together. However, we'd say the most important thing is our ability to respond flexibly to what is happening live, in the moment. For us, facilitation is a craft rather than a science - our clients come back to us because they know we can be trusted to bring presence, curiosity and appropriate playfulness to the most difficult challenges.

Viv McWaters

I once wanted to be an astronomical photographer but settled for agricultural journalist, which caused quite a hoo-ha as women weren't supposed to go to agricultural college. Rules weren't going to stop me (I had the rules changed). Now there's a clue about how I still approach life!

I worked as a journalist, and in communications, community education, training, participatory evaluation, social history and strategy development. Now I specialise in facilitation and draw on my background in the natural sciences and arts. I design workshops, conferences and training to bring them to life. I enjoy connecting people and ideas.

I studied agricultural science at Longerenong Agricultural College, and have a Bachelor of Arts in Media Studies from RMIT University, and a Masters in Applied Science (Agriculture and Rural Development) from the University of Western Sydney.

Improvisation is a constant source of inspiration, as is nature, play and the surprising things that people say and do. I have worked in over 40 different countries, mainly in south-east Asia and Africa, which has fuelled my passions for birdwatching and street art.

I live by the beach in southern Australia.

Johnnie Moore

I graduated from Oxford in Philosophy and Politics, and my early career was spent as a political researcher and speechwriter to Lord Sainsbury, then President of the UK's leading food retailing business. I moved into advertising, first as a copywriter and then as a strategic planner, working for a range of businesses from investment banks to tour operators, sportswear retailers to IT providers.

I started my own marketing consultancy in 1988, specialising in the financial services and the education sector, with an emphasis on involving customers in developing creative ideas. I did some training in humanistic psychotherapy, improvisational theatre and NLP, and my work increasingly focussed on facilitation and innovation.

As well as facilitating I am a visiting tutor on the Strategic Leadership Programme at the Saïd Business School of Oxford University.

I live in Cambridge, England and my website is www.johnniemoore.com.

Acknowledgements

Many thanks to Mary Campbell for the great design and Ferne Millen for the photos. Also to Roland Harwood, Robert Poynton, Cathy Salit, Lee Ryan and Andrew Rixon for inspiration - and all the people around the world who we've been lucky enough to work with.

creativefacilitation.com
PO Box 665
Torquay, Victoria 3228
Australia

ISBN: 9798568251491

Made in the USA
Monee, IL
15 September 2021